# Mindfulness Matters For Children

This book is dedicated to my children
Marcos, Adrian, and Samantha
my loves, my joy, my pride, with special
thanks to Marcos for helping make
my dream a reality.

# Take a Minute

1...5...10...15...20...25...30...35...40...45...50...55...60

**STOP!**

**Breathe In..........**
   **Breathe Out.........**


**Breathe In..........**
   **Breathe Out.........**

Breathe In........Feel the breath as it comes in your body

Breathe Out........Feel the breath as it leaves your body

**Breathe In...Feel the breath coming in**
**Breathe Out...Feel the breath going out**

**Breathe In...Feel the breath coming in**
**Breathe Out...Feel the breath going out**

**Breathe In...Feel the breath coming in**
**Breathe Out...Feel the breath going out**

Take The Pledge
In This Moment
I Will Stop
I Will Breathe In
I Will Breathe Out
I Will Smile

_____, I AM HERE
(your name)

Rosemary is a daughter, sister, wife, mother, grandmother, and nurse. She loves her roles and these relationships. Her desire is to empower herself, her family, and her patients to live their best life and enjoy their best health; spiritually, mentally, and physically. She teaches in Cardiopulmonary Rehabilitation and in the community on various topics including Stress Management, Mindfulness, Self-Care, and CPR. She values the importance of taking a moment in each day to be present. The present moment is a gift that you can give yourself.

Rosemary enjoys spending time with her family, reading, writing, and walking by the Mighty Mississippi River near her home.

Her mantra is "Be patient with yourself and others...Be present in each moment...Be positive in your mind and actions."

Today ...take time to breathe...to smile...to be present ...to be mindful...IT MATTERS.

CPSIA information can be obtained
at www.ICGtesting.com
Printed in the USA
LVHW010222010619
619853LV00018B/393/P